An Adventure to the International Space Station

A TRIP INTO
SPACE

Lori Haskins Houran   Illustrated by Francisca Marquez

Albert Whitman & Company
Chicago, Illinois

Taking a ride

That starts with a blast

A trip into space

Going to work—

And going there fast!

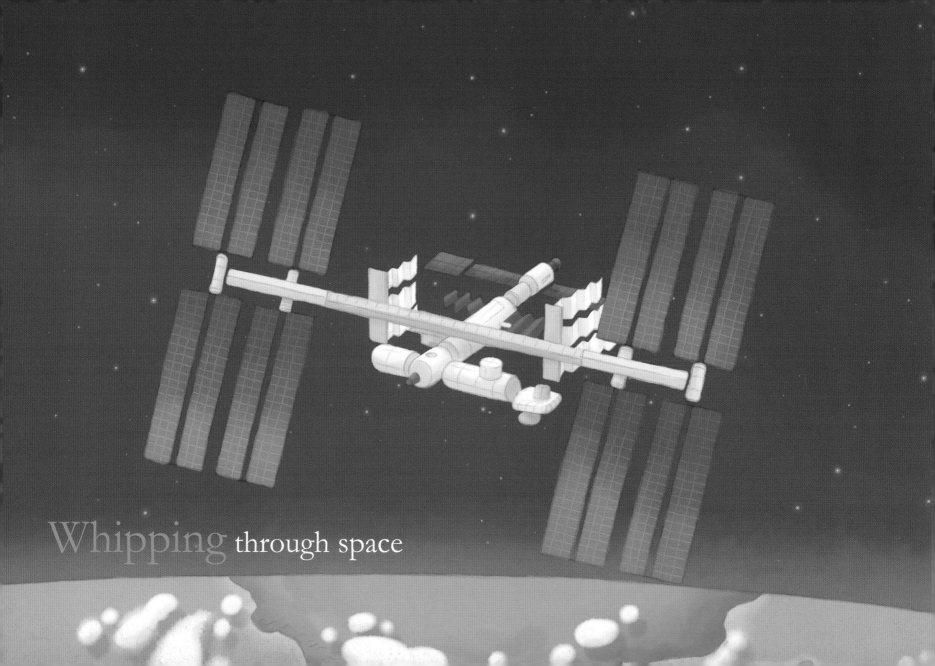

Whipping through space

Unloading boxes
And greeting the crew

Equipped out in space

Looking at Earth…

While Earth looks at you…

A blip out in space

Tasting a drink

That may float around

Taking a walk

Without any ground!

Flipping in space

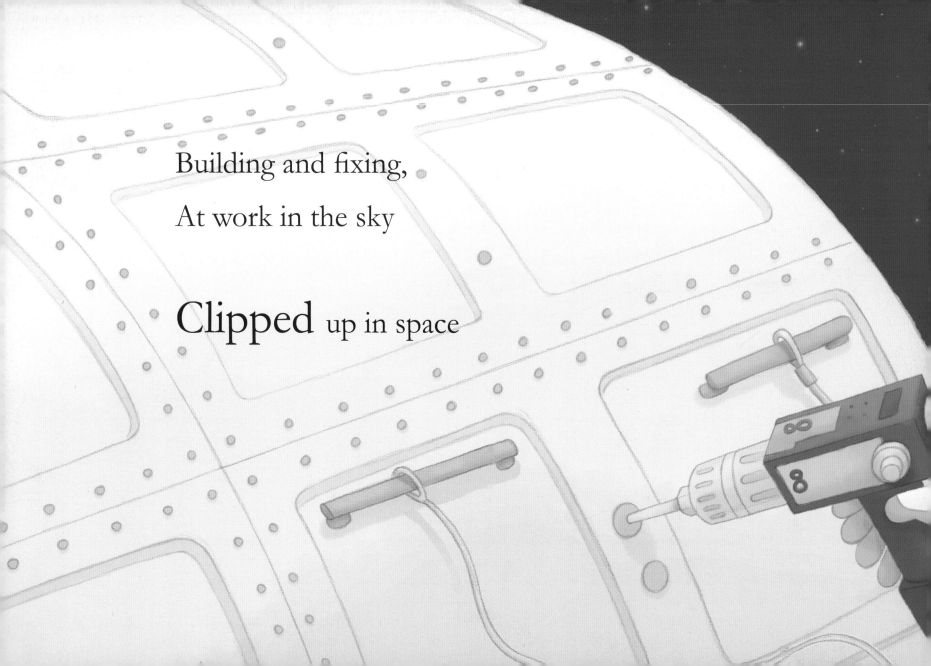

Building and fixing,

At work in the sky

Clipped up in space

Heading for bed—

Two hundred miles high!

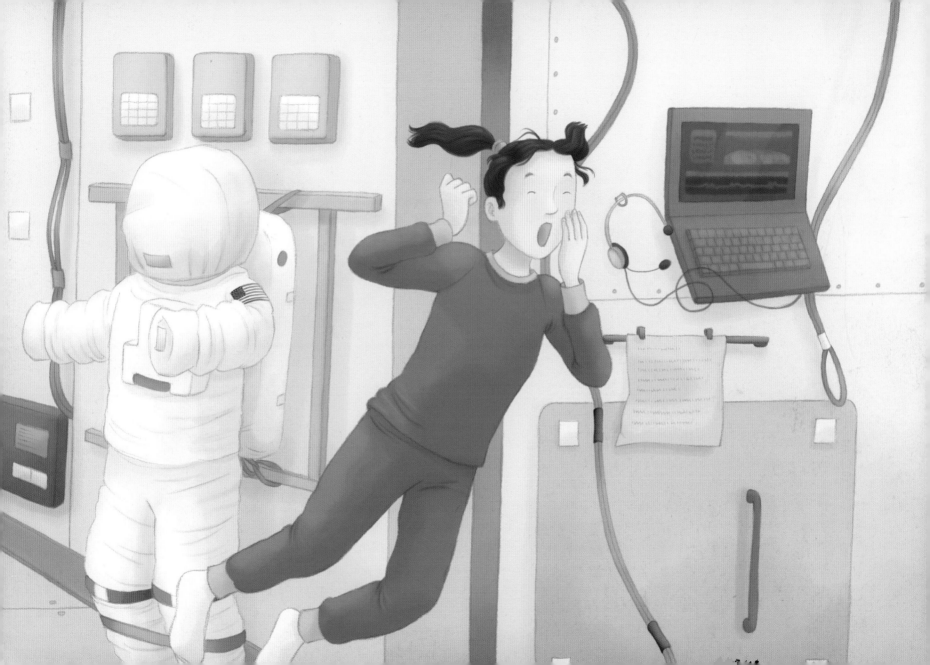

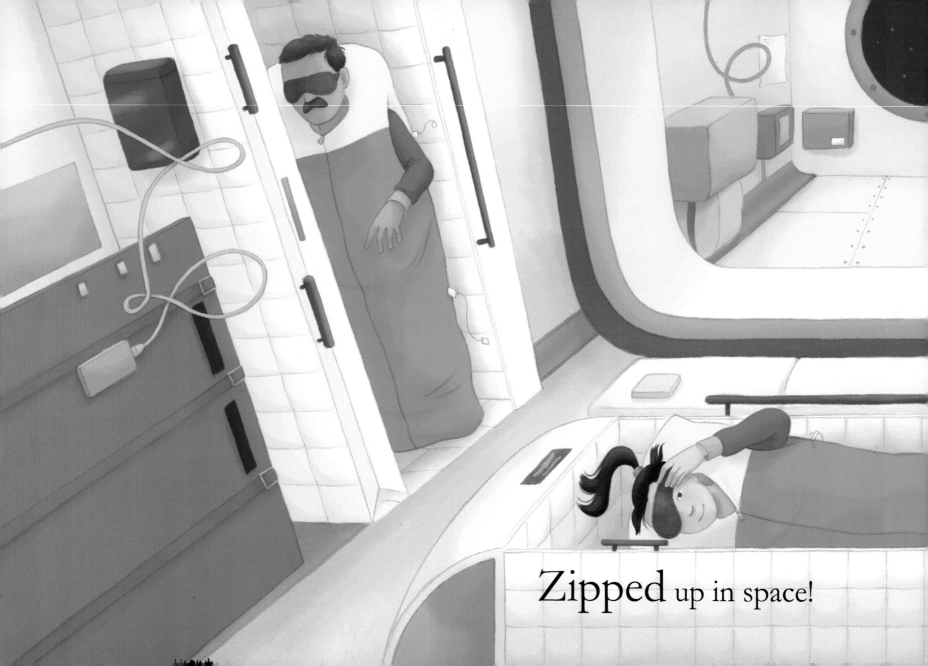

Zipped up in space!

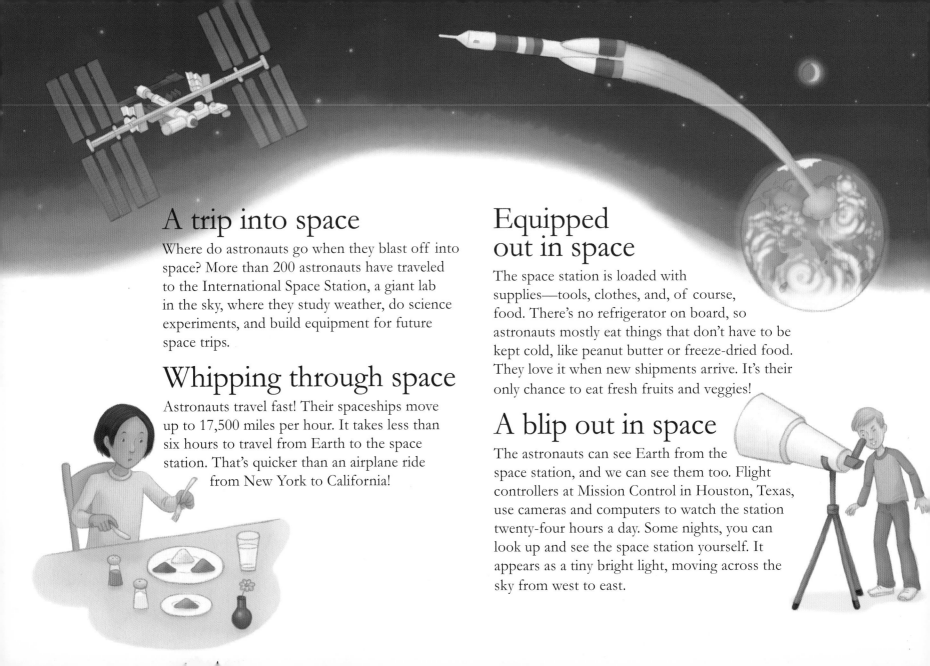

A trip into space

Where do astronauts go when they blast off into space? More than 200 astronauts have traveled to the International Space Station, a giant lab in the sky, where they study weather, do science experiments, and build equipment for future space trips.

Whipping through space

Astronauts travel fast! Their spaceships move up to 17,500 miles per hour. It takes less than six hours to travel from Earth to the space station. That's quicker than an airplane ride from New York to California!

Equipped out in space

The space station is loaded with supplies—tools, clothes, and, of course, food. There's no refrigerator on board, so astronauts mostly eat things that don't have to be kept cold, like peanut butter or freeze-dried food. They love it when new shipments arrive. It's their only chance to eat fresh fruits and veggies!

A blip out in space

The astronauts can see Earth from the space station, and we can see them too. Flight controllers at Mission Control in Houston, Texas, use cameras and computers to watch the station twenty-four hours a day. Some nights, you can look up and see the space station yourself. It appears as a tiny bright light, moving across the sky from west to east.

Sipping in space

Gravity is a powerful force that pulls things toward Earth. It keeps your feet on the ground while you're walking around. On the space station, the astronauts can't feel gravity's pull. They don't walk around—they float! Everything else floats too. Even drops of water! That's why the astronauts drink out of pouches instead of regular cups. They also use Velcro to hold down their forks between bites of food.

Flipping in space

Sometimes astronauts go on space walks to do experiments or make repairs outside the space station. The astronauts wear spacesuits that provide air to breathe and water to drink. They wear helmets with visors to protect their eyes from the sun. The visors are lined with real gold!

Clipped up in space

How do astronauts keep from floating off into space during a space walk? They're clipped to the space station with safety tethers. They also have jet packs on their backs that they can use to zoom back to the station if their safety tethers break.

Zipped up in space

Astronauts usually live at the space station for about six months at a time. They eat, work, exercise, and sleep there. To keep from floating around while they rest, the astronauts zip themselves into sleeping bags. Sleep tight!

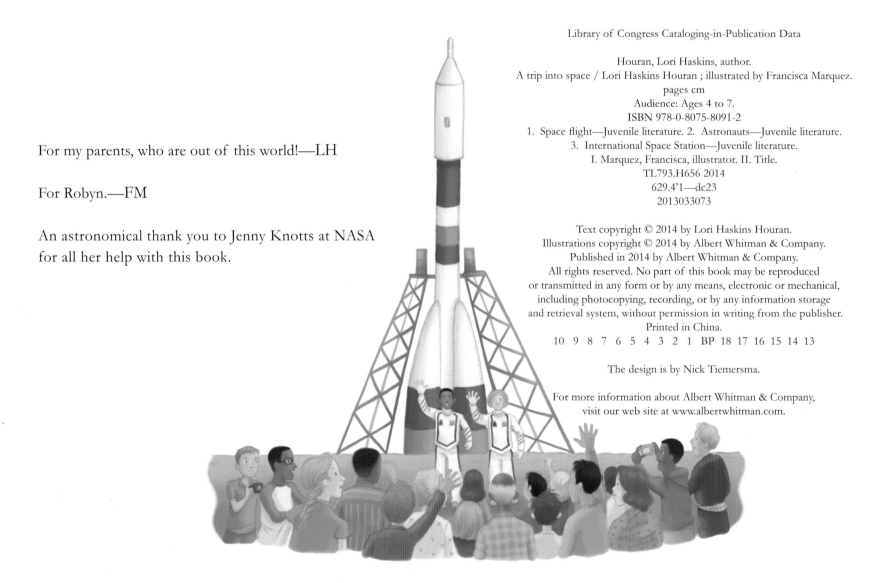

For my parents, who are out of this world!—LH

For Robyn.—FM

An astronomical thank you to Jenny Knotts at NASA
for all her help with this book.

Library of Congress Cataloging-in-Publication Data

Houran, Lori Haskins, author.
A trip into space / Lori Haskins Houran ; illustrated by Francisca Marquez.
pages cm
Audience: Ages 4 to 7.
ISBN 978-0-8075-8091-2
1. Space flight—Juvenile literature. 2. Astronauts—Juvenile literature.
3. International Space Station—Juvenile literature.
I. Marquez, Francisca, illustrator. II. Title.
TL793.H656 2014
629.4'1—dc23
2013033073

The design is by Nick Tiemersma.

For more information about Albert Whitman & Company,
visit our web site at www.albertwhitman.com.